Why, GOD?

Why, GOD?

✦

Come and See...

Joel Young

with

Danielle Young
Truman Blocker

Writers Club Press

San Jose New York Lincoln Shanghai

Why, GOD?
Come and See...

Writers Club Press
an imprint of iUniverse, Inc.

For information address:
iUniverse, Inc.
5220 S. 16th St., Suite 200
Lincoln, NE 68512
www.iuniverse.com

ISBN: 0-595-23669-3

Printed in the United States of America

Dedication

- To those just getting started, or just need to know,

- to those who have been walking with THE LORD,

- and to those who lead others to HIM.

- This book will prepare the way:

> "And it will be said: Build up, build up, prepare the way, take up/ remove the stumbling block from the way of MY people."
>
> — Isaiah 57:14

Contents

Format Note:

Questions and Answers are provided at 3 Levels

    A. For the Biblically Knowledgeable

    B. Mental/Emotional Level Answer for the growing Christian and Truth seeker

    C. Gut level response for all levels

Some questions will be a composite of the above, or focused on one particular aspect.

> "Call upon ME, and I will answer you, and I will tell you great and mighty things which you do not know"
> — Jeremiah 33:3

We did call on HIM, and here, we believe, are those answers…come and see…

ACKNOWLEDGEMENTS

To our precious LORD and SAVIOUR, to WHOM all Glory, Honor and Praise is due.

INTRODUCTION

This book will serve its purpose by answering a number of the burning questions that have been asked throughout human history.

Many have dashed their great intellects against the cliffs of ignorance without revelation from heaven above. The ways of man will never penetrate the light of heaven. Illumination comes through revelation, bringing knowledge from above.

The Truth seeker, with open mind and willing heart, will find a deep, soul satisfaction in the pages of this book. GOD will be seen in HIS Resplendent Glory. HIS Goodness, HIS Greatness, and HIS Awesome Plan, will be better apprehended and appreciated for what it truly is, as the obstacles of misunderstanding and half-truths are removed, thus preparing the way to truly see GOD.

Come and see your GOD,
and find yourself along the way.

1

WHY, GOD?
WHAT IS THE MEANING
OF LIFE?

A. WHY DID GOD CREATE US IN THE FIRST PLACE?

For Fellowship, for Relationship, for Friendship![1]

B. WHAT IS THE PURPOSE OF LIFE?

The Purpose of Life is to Glorify GOD![2]

C. WHY AM I HERE; WHAT'S THIS ALL ABOUT?

There is a plan![3] It's inside of you![4] It was placed there! You're here to share it. You're here to show it.[5] You're here to shine![6] HE has put eternity in your heart.[7]

[1]1 John 1:3,4 [2]Isaiah 43:7 [3]Jeremiah 29:11 [4]Ezekiel 36:26 [5]2 Corinthians 3:2,3 [6]Daniel 12:3 [7]Ecclesiastes 3:11

The Purpose of Life is to Glorify GOD![2]

[2]Isaiah 43:7

2

WHERE ARE YOU GOD?

A. WHERE IS GOD WHEN BAD THINGS HAPPEN?

GOD is in the Heavens (on Earth too), but HE has given the Earth to humanity.[1] It is entrusted to us to care for, to guard and to keep Planet Earth. Our KING has gone away to a far country, and will return in Glory and Power[2] to take account, to take stock in what we have done with all we've been given.[3]

B. DOES GOD CARE?

Yes GOD cares! HE has demonstrated that HE cares. HE has evidenced HIS ongoing care and concern for humanity throughout all time in all ways.[4]

C. IF GOD IS EVERYWHERE, WHY CAN'T I FIND HIM WHEN I NEED HIM?

GOD is everywhere! If we can't find HIM when we need HIM it's because we're lost—but HE's not.[5] But that's not the end of the story: HE's made a Way, and if you come to HIM in trust, and believe that GOD is WHO HE says HE is and that HE rewards those who diligently look for HIM,[6] then you will find HIM when you look for HIM with your whole heart and everything you've got.[7]

[1]Psalm 115:16 [2]Matthew 25:31-46 [3]Luke 19:12 [11-27 for context]
[4]John 3:16; Psalm 72:13,14; Psalm 116:15; 3 John 2; Romans 5:8;
Psalm 145:9 [5]Isaiah 59:1-3; Deuteronomy 28:23 [15-69 for context]
ref: *Triumph over Tragedy* (tape through For HIS Glory Ministry)
[6]Hebrews 11:6 [7]Jeremiah 29:13

> # GOD cares! HE has demonstrated that HE cares. HE has evidenced HIS ongoing care and concern for humanity throughout all time in all ways.[4]
>
> [4]John 3:16; Psalm 72:13,14; Psalm 116:15; 3 John 2; Romans 5:8; Psalm 145:9

3

THE SOVEREIGNTY OF GOD, THE SOVEREIGNTY OF MAN; ARE BOTH TRUE?

A. SINCE GOD IS SOVEREIGN, AND KNOWS ALL, ISN'T IT HIS WILL THAT I MUST GO THROUGH THIS SEVERE TRIAL/CRISIS/ SICKNESS/PAIN/PROBLEM/ETC.?

GOD is Sovereign and GOD does know all. But it is not HIS Will for us to go through these trials. GOD has sovereignly given us sovereignty over our lives. HE has made us conscious, sentient, rational beings, made in HIS Image, according to HIS Likeness,[1] just a little bit lower than HIMSELF,[2] and has placed us over all the Works of HIS Hands and has put everything under our feet.[3]

GOD's people are destroyed for lack of *the* knowledge.[4] The Hebrew Scriptures state clearly that it is not just knowledge, but *The* Knowledge, which is *The Knowledge* of GOD, that is required and desired by GOD for us and needed by man. All the treasures of The Wisdom and The Knowledge of GOD are hidden, clearly concealed, in CHRIST.[5] We also are hidden with CHRIST in GOD.[6] We are complete in CHRIST.[7]

GOD has given us authority to tread upon serpents and scorpions and over all the works of the enemy, and has said nothing by no means shall harm us.[8] This is a promise of GOD. What HE has spoken is a promise that HE keeps, yet we realize it when we keep it according to HIS Word in our lives, because HE said HE has given us the authority. Therefore we must use the authority we have been given, else it is of no avail to us. We are also told[9] that no weapon formed against us will prosper. It doesn't say that no weapon will not be formed (by the enemy) but it does state emphatically that it will not prosper, which is also to be understood: that it will not have success. If it does, then we have not used the <u>authority</u> that the Word of GOD gives us, because the rest of the verse states that "every tongue that accuses us in judgment we shall condemn."

We usually do not condemn what is wrong. We usually do not come against sin, sickness, evil, wrongdoing and speak against it; therefore it lives. GOD said it is our heritage that no weapon formed against us will prosper and that we condemn every tongue-word-authority-teaching that rises up against us. Our vindication is from THE LORD.

GOD takes us from glory to glory; not from glory to the pit.[10] GOD takes us from strength to strength[11] and GOD takes us from faith to faith.[12] GOD always leads us to triumph in CHRIST[13] and GOD has given us the victory![14] Therefore you fight *from* victory, not *for* a victory that's already won in HIM.

B. WHY IS GOD PUTTING ME THROUGH THIS?

Sin, not GOD, puts us in bad situations. Even good people suffer due to the sins of others. Babies too, suffer innocently due to The Fall of Man, which resulted in a harsh and hard world in which satan and his minions have been invited due to sin. But YESHUA/JESUS has destroyed the pain and the problems and the suffering of all mankind.

You do not have to suffer in order to learn what can be learned and what should be known without suffering. JESUS took our pain, our problems, our sicknesses, our sorrows and the sin of the world upon HIMSELF and off us.

The penalty of sin was paid by HIM, clearing us, giving us real peace in HIM.

YESHUA/JESUS is the answer! HE paid it all in full!

C. HOW COULD A **GOOD GOD** DO THIS TO ME?

HE couldn't. And HE didn't! GOD IS GOOD. GOD IS KIND. GOD IS CARING! And GOD IS LOVE! And GOD doesn't change!

[1]Genesis 1:26,27 [2]Psalm 8:5 [3]Psalm 8:6 [4]Hosea 4:6 [5]Colossians 2:3 [6]Colossians 3:3 [7]Colossians 2:10 [8]Luke 10:19 [9]Isaiah 54:17 [10]2 Corinthians 3:17 [11]Psalm 84:7(verse 8 in Hebrew) [12]Romans 1:17 [13]2 Corinthians 2:14 [14]1 Corinthians 15:57

GOD always leads us to triumph in CHRIST[13] and GOD has given us the victory![14] Therefore you fight *from* victory, not *for* a victory that's already won in HIM.

[13]2 Corinthians 2:14 [14]1 Corinthians 15:57

4

DO I NEED TO BE SICK, SAD, OR SUFFER, TO BE A SAINT?

A: WHEN BAD THINGS HAPPEN, WHO'S TO BLAME?

It's up to you! Many people, when bad things happen to them, seek to assign blame. Who's to blame? There are only four possibilities that fit this bill. Is it GOD, satan, others, or themselves? Let's address each one from a causative point of view.

First, when you truly know GOD, HIS Character, HIS Essence, HIS Nature, you know that HE is All Good, All GOD, and always Right. There is no darkness in HIM.[1] There is no concord between Good and evil, of Light with darkness, or of CHRIST with Belial.[2]

Second, satan will attempt to influence, lure, trap, and tempt people in every possible way. However, it is not possible when one chooses GOD, not satan, and walks in the newness of Life of THE SPIRIT. Armed with the full armor of GOD,[3] leading a crucified life, walking as JESUS walked, you will walk like a son or daughter of GOD on Earth in total victory.

Third, others may be a source of harm to themselves and/or people at large. They use their will against themselves, even against others. They are accountable. However, if and when the Christian walks on

Earth like JESUS, not only should no harm come to them, but they should be able to prevent the evil expression.

Lastly, oneself. Ultimately, as difficult as this is for some to stomach, we are responsible for our World, our life, and our brothers.[4] When something bad happens in the World, though the people perpetrating evil are directly responsible for their own actions, we have, by ignorance,[5] or the slothfulness of the soul,[6] or lack of unity,[7] or lack of trust,[8] or by lack of faith,[9] or lack of knowing who we are in CHRIST,[10] or lack of love,[11] created an environment for evil's expression.

We can already hear the outcry of some: "But I pray", "I read my BIBLE", "I go to Church", "I tithe", and so on. We thank GOD, truly, for all you do. It's good, but we need to do much more. We have only to look around the World to see the need, which must be at least met to be stopped, and more than met to be conquered. In CHRIST, we are more than conquerors. But we must become who we truly are.

Why do you think you must go to school some 20 years to become a doctor (before specializing) to minister healing to the masses, learning a specialized language and techniques, but we can pray almost any old way and expect instant results? Even high school takes 12 years for a minimum competency, and that is well accepted and understood by all. Even to be involved in Real Estate, Insurance sales, you need to study, learn, and be tested to meet competency standards, which could take months. How much time have we devoted to become effective Christians? What courses of study have we taken to be Biblically competent Christians? What does your course of study look like on a daily, weekly, monthly, yearly basis?[12]

Being a Christian for 20 years does not mean we've devoted 20 years to being a Christian. Please hear what we say, in love; the Truth. Don't blame anyone else anymore. Let's make a serious change now, and take CHRIST seriously. HE believes in us; let's believe in the us HE believes in.

B/C: DON'T WE LEARN FROM BAD THINGS? ISN'T GOD TRYING TO TEACH ME SOMETHING BY ALLOWING THIS BAD THING TO HAPPEN TO ME, JUST LIKE PAUL? ISN'T THIS MY "THORN IN THE FLESH"? ISN'T THIS MY "CROSS TO BEAR"?

GOD made you good, GOD made you great, GOD made you just like HIM; just a little lower.[13] GOD took all your pain and suffering on a cross some 2000 years ago,[14] even from the foundation of the world[15] so you don't have to suffer, so you don't have to be in pain, so you don't have to be sick, poor, or have sorrow.

GOD has told us that SCRIPTUREs are all GOD breathed (inspired). And that they are profitable for teaching, for instructing us,[16] for reproof, for correction, for training us in righteousness, that we may be adequate, equipped for every good work.[17] GOD gave us SCRIPTUREs to teach us, not problems. GOD gave us SCRIPTUREs to instruct us, not the world. GOD gave us SCRIPTUREs to reprove/rebuke/admonish us, not satan!

GOD gave us SCRIPTUREs for correcting us, not crises. GOD gave SCRIPTUREs for training us in righteousness, not the temptations of the world.

GOD says that the SCRIPTURE has made us adequate, equipping us for every good work. Thus falsifying the inane position that we need problems, pain, punishment, or sickness, etc. to be our "teacher". GOD has given us HIS WORD. It is all sufficient. It is complete. It is GOD breathed, giving us life, and life more abundantly.[18]

Further, THE FATHER and THE SON has sent us THE HOLY SPIRIT to be our TEACHER, not satan! If satan and sickness are our "teachers", then you deny THE TEACHER, THE HOLY SPIRIT. And don't even think to do that—Please!

What about Paul's "thorn in the flesh",[19] you say. I know what THE BIBLE says, it's "in the flesh". Sounds painful to me. Further, Paul prayed three times for release of this "thorn in the flesh" and he still had it. What about that?

Hold your seats—let's look at the whole BIBLE—in context. First, recognize that Paul was a Jew. He spoke like a Jew, he thought like a Jew, and he wrote often in Jewish terms. This expression "thorn in the flesh" is a <u>Hebrew idiom</u>, unknown to most as such. It has nothing to do with the physical body, the flesh, or any bodily illness or sickness whatsoever. It is an idiom not unlike idioms of any culture. (eg: "kick the bucket", "break a leg", "he's a pain in the neck", "he gets on my nerves", etc.). If one turns to Numbers 33:55 and Joshua 23:13, to give you two examples[20] you will clearly see the same core essence expressed idiomatically, that people are the "thorn in the flesh", not a physical sickness or illness. Further, in the Text itself, the next immediate clause tells you that the "thorn in the flesh" is a "messenger of satan". Make no mistake about it; the "thorn in the flesh" is not in the flesh. It is a messenger of satan attacking and harassing Paul at every opportunity and by all possible means.

What about Paul's prayer? Paul entreated THE LORD three times that it might depart from him.[21] GOD said: "MY Grace is sufficient for you, for power is perfected in weakness."[22]

Sufficient: is an old word of rich meaning "to ward off against danger",[23] CHRIST's Grace suffices and abides—the term sufficient, The Greek *arke'o* has the idea of raising a barrier, to ward off, (ie: by implication to avail, figuratively to be satisfactory—be content, be enough, suffice, be sufficient). The word *arke'o* is akin to the word *airo* which means to lift, by implication, to take up and away, to raise (voice). *Arke'o* means to be possessed of unfailing strength, to suffice, to be enough, (as against any danger, hence to defend, to ward off). Thus

GOD's Grace is strong enough and sufficient enough to defend one against the messenger's of satan but being raised up as a barrier, and thus is able to ward off any danger.

"Power": *dunamis*, means inherent power, being able or capable. "In weakness": in the Greek is the term *en asthenaya*, means to be of sickness or weakness, and is the most common expression for sickness and are used in the comprehensive sense of the whole man.[24] Further,[25] *asthenaya* means "want of strength", "weakness", "infirmity"…of body…feebleness of health, sickness…of soul, want of strength, incapacity, requisite…then, relative to our verse, in[26] "the mental states in which this weakness manifests itself". Then following, Thayer[25] states in the next verse,[27] "when I am weak in human strength, then I am strong in divine strength".

"Is perfected" *talaytie*: "to be made perfect or complete" only in the sense of reaching one's "prescribed goal"[28] Scholar A. T. Robertson,[29] states "of *teleo*: to finish. It is linear in idea. Power is continually increased as the weakness grows. In Trench,[30] with reference to the Greek term for Grace, *charis*, came to signify in the New Testament "the Favor, the Grace and the Goodness of GOD to man." In New Testament usage, *charis* denotes the Grace of The Worthy to the unworthy and of THE HOLY to the unholy.[31]

Thus, what do we have so far? We have a perpetuating attack of a messenger of satan against Paul. He prays for the removal of this messenger of satan—"thorn in the flesh". GOD's answer to him is "MY Favor, MY Grace, MY Goodness, is raised up as a barrier for you. To ward off, to avail for you, and thus be satisfactory enough, sufficient for you, to now be possessed of unfailing strength, to be strong, to suffice for you, to be enough against any danger. Thus to defend you and to ward off for you."

Thus Paul, GOD's Grace is ever strong enough and thus sufficient enough to defend you by being raised as a barrier and thus able to ward off any danger for you. For power is perfected in weakness. GOD's inherent power, ability, capability will be continually increased as the weakness grows. It is made perfect or complete only in the sense of reaching one's prescribed goal. For in my weakness, the Power of THE MESSIAH will overshadow me in the sense of CHRIST abiding upon me as a tent spread over me during my temporary stay on Earth.

For the compound verb, *episkaynosey*, means to "fix a tent or habitation upon".[32] Thus, Paul well understands now that even in his weakness, GOD's Power will help make him perfect or complete helping him reach his prescribed goal. During that time, as he ministers for CHRIST's sake, he can be well content in weaknesses and insults and distresses and persecutions and difficulties, because The Power of CHRIST will help him reach his prescribed goal as it overshadows him like a tent spread over him during his temporary stay on Earth. Thus, he can say that when he is weak, he is not weak, but in his weakness he is strong. For CHRIST's Power overshadows him, perfecting him, helping him reach his prescribed goal and completing his race. When you are weak, then you are strong when you rely on HIS Strength, Power, and Ability.

Note well Psalm 23:5 which states "THOU preparest a table before me in the presence of my enemies..." Further, the same theme is picked up in Psalm 110:2 "THE LORD will send forth YOUR strong scepter from Zion, saying: "Rule in the midst of THINE enemies".

[1]1 John 1:5 [2]2 Corinthians 6:14,15 [3]Ephesians 6:10-17 [4]Psalm 115:16 [5]Hosea 4:6 [6]Philippians 3:14 [7]John 17:23; Ephesians 4:3 [8]Proverbs 3:5,6 [9]Luke 18:8 [10]Psalm 8:5,6; Luke 10:19; Isaiah 54:17; Romans 8:37; 2 Corinthians 2:14; 1 Corinthians 15:57 [11]John 13:34,35 [12]1 Peter 3:15,16 [13]Psalm 8:5 [14]John 19:30 [15]Revelation 13:8 [16]2 Timothy 3:16 [17]2 Timothy 3:17 [18]John 10:10b [19]2 Corinthians 12:7 [20]Deuteronomy 19:15 [21]2 Corinthians 12:8 [22]2 Corinthians 12:9 [23] ref A. T. Robertson WPNT, Vol 4 p266 [24]ref *The*

Complete Word Study New Testament BIBLE by Spiros, Zodhiates p881 in the *Lexical Aids to the New Testament* [25] in Thayer's *Greek-English Lexicon of the NT*, p80 [26]2 Corinthians 12:9 [27]2 Corinthians 12:10 [28]*The Complete Word Study New Testament BIBLE* by Spiros, Zodhiates p948 in the *Lexical Aids to the New Testament.* [29] in his *Word Pictures in the New Testament*, Vol 4, p266 [30]*Synonyms of the New Testament* p181 [31]Ibid. p182 [32]Vincent's *Word Study of the New Testament* p356

When you truly know GOD, HIS Character, HIS Essence, HIS Nature, you know that HE is All Good, All GOD, and always Right.

There is no darkness in HIM.[1]

[1]1 John 1:5

5

DOES GOD ANSWER PRAYER?

A: WHY DOESN'T GOD ANSWER MY PRAYERS? DOESN'T HE HEAR ME?

To answer the second part first: "Doesn't HE hear me?" the answer is yes—and no. What is often missing to the English reader is an understanding of the original language of THE BIBLE: Hebrew. The Hebrew word for hear is based on a three-letter root *shama*. What is most interesting about this word and necessary for you to know is that the root word for hear[1] also means obey. Therefore to hear is to obey; these are two inseparable concepts, two sides of the same coin. Therefore, when we pray, if it is in accordance with HIS Will, Character, and Essence, then HE hears the prayer and obeys it. Does GOD obey our prayer? The question is better stated that GOD keeps HIS OWN WORD. When HE hears HIS WORD, HIS NATURE, being spoken by HIS saints, it has become HIS WORD in them that HE is watching over it to perform.[2]

Often when we pray, we pray asking GOD to do what HE has already done. JESUS has said: "It is finished!"[3] Further, our LORD, THE LAMB of GOD, has been slain from the foundation of the world.[4] This has tremendous implications. For, before there was a sinner, there was THE SAVIOUR. Before there was a problem, there was THE SOLUTION. Before there was a question on what to do, there

19

was THE ANSWER. Thus, it is necessary to realize that we often pray wrongly for GOD to do what HE has already done. This approach, as many will painfully note, does not work. There is a science to THE SPIRIT that surpasses any and all of the natural sciences in detail and depth. We must not be casual or naïve in the things of THE SPIRIT for there is a law to THE SPIRIT and an order in the things of GOD.[5]

Many go to school or study various trades for years in order to achieve a certain measure of competency. Further, they continue to perfect their skills and grow in knowledge in their chosen field. This is a process that requires serious commitment. How much more in the matters of GOD! More than the difference between appendicitis and tonsillitis to both surgeon and layperson, is the difference between mere words and true prayer in the science of GOD. We must learn and show ourselves approved to GOD.[6] We must be true learners/disciples of JESUS CHRIST[7]

Further, we must learn how to pray the Way GOD would have us to pray—with the same mind, with the same passion, with the same plan, and with the same purpose. We must stop asking for GOD to Bless us when HE has already done so.[8] We must stop wondering if the Promises of GOD are "Yes", "no", "maybe", or "later". GOD has said that no matter how many promises HE has made they are "Yes!" in HIM,[9] not "no". HE has said "YES", therefore, it is not "no". HE has said "YES" which doesn't mean "maybe". HE has said "YES", which doesn't mean "later", because "later" means "no" now.

Further, it must be understood that "later" means "suffer now" with whatever you are praying about. Does that sound like a GOOD GOD? Not our GOD! GOD is GOOD and HIS Loyal LOVE is forever.[10] GOD is good to all (which includes you) and HIS Tender Mercies are over all HIS Works.[11]

Many people pray in unbelief. They're hoping for, but not believing in, they're wishing for something to happen, but not believing that it's already done. What does that mean, "it's already done"? This has all too often been a missing piece in prayer. We are told by JESUS HIM-SELF to *have faith in GOD*, to *believe in GOD*, to *trust in GOD*. HE has *instructed* us[12] to believe that we have received it already. This is usually delinquent in both our prayers and in our heart.

We all too often and always incorrectly pray for something that we don't have, just like we don't have it. JESUS said otherwise. JESUS said to pray believing, trusting HIM that you do have it already; and don't waver, be steadfast in your heart. Don't watch your watch, watch GOD. Don't watch the circumstances, watch CHRIST. Don't be moved by what you see or hear or feel; only by what you believe. And true belief is in the TRUTH of THE TRUE GOD. We seek for things to happen in the future; but GOD said to seek for the future in the past. We seek for things to happen in the present—but GOD said to seek for them also in the past too.[13] This is all too often a very strange concept for the prayer, only because we are unfamiliar with the Ways of GOD.

We all live on a time line here on Earth that goes forward from the past to the present to the future. Most remember the past; all experience the present, yet few remember the future. Why not? The prophets did. Our false beliefs have locked us into unbelieving prayers that cannot be answered because they are contrary to the Truth. This is not to say it is an issue of heart-felt sincerity. But GOD said HIS people perish for lack of *The* Knowledge,[14] not for lack of sincerity. Some have said: "well, my friend is a GODly person and they prayed and they still suffer and they're still in pain". But this perspective fails, because only GOD is fully GODly, and HE sets the standard of GODliness completely.

All of us humans that know HIM are growing into some measure of GODliness according to the standard of GODliness that HE has set in CHRIST.[15] Now realize that GOD has already answered every prayer and every petition for everything. HE has already provided salvation for every soul, healing for every body, and peace and composure to every mind and heart. HE has already answered every prayer, HIS prayers.

Then why pray? It doesn't change GOD since HE doesn't change.[16] If GOD doesn't change, then why pray? *You must change.* And the way to change is through prayer because prayer changes you! Prayer causes you to change, to take the shape of the answer you need.

Prayer exercises your soul and mind to conform to HIS, to receive what HE has already given, as you believe what HE has already done; as done. You start to think like GOD, you start to act like GOD, you start to be who you are in GOD to the degree your prayer and your walk shapes you into HIS Image. This is a lifetime and an ongoing process.

This is why we're told to pray without ceasing.[17] True prayer enables me to think like GOD, to believe in what GOD believes in, and to become what GOD has said I am in GOD. GOD is for you, and with HIM has freely given you all things.[18] You must believe in GOD, and believe that GOD believes in you. You need to believe in the you that HE believes in now. Amen!

B: WHY DON'T MY PRAYERS WORK?

The first thing to do is to pray according to HIS Will.[19] In order to truly know GOD's Will, you need to know GOD's Character, because will and character are ultimately inseparable. One of the key ways to know GOD's Character is to know the meaning of HIS NAMEs. (ref: For HIS Glory NAMEs of GOD tape series—www.ForHISGlory.org) There are hundreds of attributive NAMEs for GOD, each One describing a facet of WHO HE IS.

A name basically connotes three things: essence, identity, and nature. Therefore, as we begin to know GOD through HIS NAMEs, we begin to know HIS Character. When we begin to know HIS Character, we will begin to know what HIS Will is.

When you truly know what HIS Will is, you can pray to GOD without doubt in your heart. Make no mistake about it, two key reasons prayers do not work, is when we do not pray according to HIS Will, and/or when we have doubt in our heart.

C: DOES GOD CARE?

Yes! GOD cares! HE thinks about you all the time. HE has a Great Plan for you. HE has sent you HIS best GIFT possible to you: JESUS! Accept the GIFT, and watch your life change. Refuse the GIFT, and you're on your own. The choice is yours. You may choose not to believe in GOD, but GOD believes in you. You may choose not to love GOD, but GOD Loves you, no matter what you do. You may turn away from GOD, but GOD does not turn away from you. Come to HIM and see...

[1]Deuteronomy 6:4; Genesis 3:8; Genesis 3:17; Deuteronomy 4:30 [2]Jeremiah 1:12 [3]John 19:30 [4]Revelation 13:8 [5]Romans 8:2; 1 Corinthians 14:33 [6]2 Timothy 2:15 [7]Matthew 28:18-20; John 8:31:32; 2 Peter 3:18 [8]Ephesians 1:3 [9]2 Corinthians 1:20 [10]Psalm 136:1 [11]Psalm 145:9 [12]Mark 11:24 [22-24] [13]Ecclesiastes 3:15 [14]Hosea 4:6 [15]Ephesians 4:13 [16]Malachi 3:6a; Hebrews 13:8; James 1:17 [17]1 Thessalonians 5:17 [18]Romans 8:31,32 [19]1 John 5:14,15

GOD has said that no matter how many promises HE has made they are "Yes!" in HIM,[9] not "no". HE has said "YES", therefore, it is not "no". HE has said "YES" which doesn't mean "maybe". HE has said "YES", which doesn't mean "later", because "later" means "no" now.

[9] 2 Corinthians 1:20

Many people pray in unbelief.
They're hoping for, but not
believing in, they're wishing for
something to happen, but not
believing that it's already done.
What does that mean,
"it's already done"?
This has all too often been a
missing piece in prayer.
We are told by
JESUS HIMSELF
to have faith in GOD,
to believe in GOD,
to trust in GOD.

HE has *instructed* us[12]
to believe that
we have received it already.

[12]Mark 11:24 [22-24]

6

DOES GOD "ALLOW" BAD THINGS TO HAPPEN?

A: DOES GOD "ALLOW" BAD THINGS TO HAPPEN?

The force of this question is better understood by understanding this: It is really we who allow, due to *our choice*, what kind of life we live. If we choose life, then we will live the life of CHRIST JESUS.[1] If we choose death, then we will be among the living dead[2], just like satan and the fallen angels. It is important to make the following distinction: having free will gives us the opportunity to choose, by an act of will, to live life, and to live it right. We need not sin. We need not ever sin. Adam, both of them,[3] were sinless until they sinned.

JESUS expects us not to sin anymore.[4] If we do, there is remedy: the Blood of JESUS.[5] Important to note, is that angels, also at one point in their history, has a choice to make: to stay loyal to GOD or to follow satan in a cosmic act of rebellion against THE MOST HIGH GOD. Remember carefully, though one-third of the angels followed satan and sinned through rebellion, two-thirds did not and stayed loyal to their GOD. We make the decision, just as they have also.

We have searched a number of Biblical sources, including *Strongs' Exhaustive Concordance, The Blue Letter Bible* on the Internet, the *Franklin NIV Version Computer Bible, Vines Complete Expository Dictionary,* **Bible Works 4.0** software, and there is no evidence to support the fact that GOD allows sin, sickness, evil, or The Fall of man. In actual point of fact, GOD did not allow any of these, and you can make no Biblical case for GOD allowing bad things to happen.

Quite the contrary, when you look up the word allow/permit in its varied forms, you'll see, all too often, it is what we permit and allow that gets us into trouble, not GOD. For example: "the nations you will dispossess listened to those who practice sorcery or divination. But as for you, THE LORD your GOD has not permitted you to do so."[6] How do you explain then, when we see Jews (and not only Jews) practicing sorcery and listening to psychics, fortunetellers, shamans, etc? Who allowed that? GOD said HE did not! Then who did? Answer: we did! We are seeing something in this world that GOD did not permit. However, it exists in this world. Don't miss this point. This is a startling revelation, that we are seeing something in this world that GOD expressly said that HE did not permit you to do. Then how could it exist? Then how could it be? Answer: we brought it in to existence; we brought sin into the world through disobedience. Therefore, we are permitting it to be, not GOD. By the exercise of our willful choice, we allow what we allow.

> "Yet the children of your people say, the way of THE LORD is not proper; rather, it is their way which is not proper".
> — Ezekiel 33:17

The gift of the Freedom of Choice is one that's imbued with responsibility. To whom much is given, much is required, but to whom much is required, much has been given to meet the requirement. Choices make us who we are. GOD made us who we are to be. Choose GOD. Choose wisely.

Take it seriously!

[1]John 1:4; John 8:12; John 10:10 [2]Revelation 20:11-15 [3]Genesis 1:26-27; Genesis 3:20; Genesis 5:2 [4]1 John 2:1; John 8:11 [5]1 John 2:1; 1 John 1:9 [6]Deuteronomy 18:14

> It is really we who allow, due to our choice, what kind of life we live. If we choose life, then we will live the life of CHRIST JESUS.[1]
>
> [1]John 1:4; John 8:12; John 10:10

7

DOES A SOVEREIGN GOD PERMIT BAD THINGS TO HAPPEN, OR DO WE?

A: How is a Sovereign GOD implicated in the wrongs of the world through HIS permissive Will?

Let's first examine the word allow/permit /let/suffer... It is our position that you will find not one verse in the entire BIBLE that says "GOD permitted", or "GOD allowed" any problem whatsoever. We wrongly view the world through our limited myopic vision and personal experience.[1] We set ourselves up as both judge and jury of both events and people, and unfortunately, unwittingly, of GOD HIMSELF. This will never do.

There is one standard, set by ONE WHO is HIMSELF that STANDARD. One set of laws, established as expressions of THAT BEING from whence we all came. One ultimate Perfect Plan, that has both fully apprehended and fully comprehended all that man could, would, and should and shouldn't do, yet has made all that is contrary to GOD HIMSELF obedient to GOD HIMSELF, ultimately.

Even that which opposes HIS Will, being apprehended by GOD HIMSELF in HIS timeless eternity, will not deny HIS Perfect Plan from being expressed and manifested by those who freely choose to love HIM. Whereas those who choose not to love HIM, will express their own will and their own plan within the limitations that GOD has set for evil. Thus giving people their own will contrary to his ideal plan for them.

GOD has desired fellowship, and thus created beings like HIM-SELF but not HIMSELF, giving them the right to love and live, or not. Some have said "yes"…many have said "no". They chose not to love but to hate, not to live but to die. In their death, they live forever as dead, the living dead, gods of their own decision, gods of their own hell. GOD did not allow this, GOD did not choose this, and GOD did not want this! But HE has given us our own will to will, our own choice to choose. HE has told us what to choose, yet the choice is up to us. It has always been, it is ever so.

B: WHY DOES GOD PERMIT BAD THINGS TO HAPPEN, OR DOES HE?

Who said HE does? Did GOD allow Adam to fall? HIS instructions were: "do not eat of the tree of knowledge of good and evil!"[2] Did GOD allow Moses to strike the rock when HE specifically said just to speak to it, and thus incur personal sin keeping him out of the Promised Land after decades of service?

Did GOD allow Dinah to be raped? Be very careful, very careful how you talk and think about GOD! Did GOD permit all of the babies in Bethlehem to be slaughtered by Herod? Did GOD permit Hitler to wreak havoc to the millions, and Stalin even more so? What about the anti-christ/anti-messiah yet to come who will be the worst of them all by far? What about them, what about them all?

Let's look at the last case first, the anti-christ. With all the studies on Revelation that have been done, as to the identity of the anti-christ, we propose a more definitive and exacting question: "Why an anti-christ?" This question has all too sadly been rarely asked, and less answered.

Why an anti-christ? The answer is two-fold. First, it meets the desire of the people who don't desire CHRIST. This is hard to fathom for many, yet one's desire is a very powerful force.

Desire strongly influences will and one's decision-making processes. Spiritual desire is the strongest desire of the human being. When one rejects GOD and HIS SPIRIT, that desire still desires to be met. It never ceases to amaze us the horrific substitutes for GOD that people so easily and cheaply fall prey too. Trojan horses are still ever present and have been swallowed into the cities of the mind by many of our fellow human beings.

People who reject GOD end up looking for a god somewhere else. But that somewhere is nowhere and that someone isn't GOD.

Second, when we reject CHRIST as LORD and SAVIOUR we, with the same decision, make a contract with evil, an agreement with sheol, a covenant with death[3] Thus, one immediately has turned his face towards the darkness, toward evil, away from the light, ever into the night, which never ends.[4]

C: HOW COULD A GOOD GOD LET BAD THINGS HAPPEN TO US?

Remember, from Chapter 3, (WHO's in Charge Anyway?) that it is not HIS Will, nor is it HIS desire for you to be hurt, harmed, or not healed, etc. GOD is Good! And THE BIBLE says that HIS Goodness is extended over everything HE has Made.

GOD also doesn't change. Which means HE is always Good. Don't blame GOD for bad things. Thank GOD for all the Good that HE does. Don't look at GOD as someone WHO is against you, or will hurt you.

GOD has only good intentions for you. If someone were to do what we accuse GOD of doing, we would put him in jail. Don't paint people out to be better than GOD; that's not good and that's not right.

[1]1 Corinthians 13:11,12 [2]Genesis 2:17 [3]Isaiah 28:15 [4]John 5:43

GOD doesn't change. .
HE is always Good.
Don't blame GOD for bad
things. Thank GOD for all
the Good that HE does.
Don't look at GOD as
someone WHO is against you,
GOD has only good intentions
for you. If someone were to
do what we accuse GOD of
doing, we would put him in jail.
Don't paint people out to be
better than GOD.

8

HOW COULD A GOOD GOD CREATE PEOPLE KNOWING THAT MANY WOULD BE LOST IN HELL FOREVER?

A: SINCE GOD KNEW THIS ALL AHEAD OF TIME (FOREKNOWLEDGE), WHY WOULD A LOVING, GOOD GOD CREATE PEOPLE SO THAT MOST OF THEM WOULD END UP IN HELL?

An excellent question, one that many serious students and scholars alike have wrestled with over the years. Many have gone off the path by misunderstanding critical topics such as predestination and Sovereignty. Others will cast the blame on the people going to hell saying that the decision is theirs, and theirs alone. This again falls far short of an adequately acceptable answer. The question remains unanswered at this point still, because the question is not do people end up in hell based on their own choice, but why would a Loving, Good GOD knowing what they would choose from the perspective of a timeless eternity, still choose to create people, knowing that most of them[1] would end up in hell.

Even if one person would end up in hell, the question remains: Why, GOD? For it is not a question of quantity but of quality and character, the very Character of GOD. Let's address the issues carefully, one at a time.

Predestination: For whom HE did foreknow, HE also predestined to be conformed to the Image of HIS SON, that HE might be the first born among many brethren[2] Moreover, whom HE did predestine, HE also called, and those HE called, HE also justified, and those HE justified, HE also glorified.[3]

HE predestined us to the adoption as sons through JESUS CHRIST to HIMSELF, according to the kind intention of HIS Will.[4] Also we have obtained an inheritance, having been predestined according to HIS Purpose WHO Works all things after the Counsel of HIS OWN Will.[5]

Sovereignty: GOD is Sovereign. GOD is LORD over all.[6] THE LORD is in The Heavens, HE does whatever HE pleases[7]. Do you know the ordinances of Heaven? Can you establish its dominion on Earth?[8] GOD IS GOD. GOD is THE GOD OF GODs and THE LORD OF LORDs.[9] GOD alone is GOD.

B: Since GOD knows all things ahead of time, why would a Loving Good GOD create people in the first place, knowing that most of them would end up in hell?

In GOD's Foreknowledge, HE knew what everyone would choose. GOD has chosen for us the best: the good of the land, good health, long life, family, a future and a hope. HE has chosen peace for us, and not evil.[10] HE has also told us what to choose: life, not death; health, not sickness; good, not evil, blessings, not curses.[11]

In GOD's Foreknowledge, HE knew there would be some who would choose HIS Plan for them and there would be others who would not. JESUS HIMSELF tells us[12] that the way is broad and the gate is wide that leads to destruction, and many are those who find it = choose it. Then, The Way is straight and The Gate is narrow to life, few there are who find it = choose it.

A common answer is that man chooses to obey his destiny and believe in GOD, or that a man chooses to disobey his destiny in GOD, and act as a god himself in deciding his own destiny, thus disobeying GOD.[13] It is our choice! The natural outcome of this is that the person who obeys GOD through JESUS CHRIST will see life, experience life, and have life, and that life more abundantly.[14] Whereas, the person who disobeys GOD and thus denies his own true destiny, does not see life, does not experience true life, but becomes a shade of existence, a shadow, darkness itself.

Yet the question still remains in front of us. For the force of the question, does not question man's choice, but GOD's decision-making through HIS Foreknowledge with respect to HIS unchanging Character.[15] That Character exhibits, among other Divine Attributes: Love, Goodness, and Holiness.

GOD gives you what you want, within the parameters of HIS Divine Plan, to which all things have been apprehended and comprehended, and made subject to. GOD gives you what you want, since The Decision to choose has been given to you. HE has sovereignly given us sovereignty over our actions, choices, thoughts, and lives. HE has told us what to do.[16] The decision is ours. HE will confirm your decision, affirming your right to choose what you choose, but not choosing the choice for us. GOD gives you what you want.

Not everyone wants to go to Heaven! Does this surprise you? It surprises us, and equally saddens us. However, JESUS has told us all this already. That even though Light has come into the world, men loved the darkness rather that the Light for their deeds were evil. JESUS noted that everyone doing evil hates the Light and doesn't come to the Light for fear that his deeds would be exposed.[17] GOD in HIS Mercy has put a limit to evil, thank GOD!

Further, interestingly, is the fact that not only will evil be judged in ultimate categories by our LORD when HE sits in Judgment over HIS Creation; but, even now, the darkness is passing away.[18] An understanding of the Greek middle voice sheds tremendous light on this clause in this passage in 1 John.[18] For the Greek grammar of the middle voice tells us the subject of the verb *is acting upon itself.*

Therefore, the darkness contains within itself the seed of its own destruction, and thus it is in and of itself passing away through its own actions. This[19] is an amazing design principle by GOD through HIS Divine Plan, in which HE makes evil both subject to HIS Divine Plan and subjected to destruction via its own actions. Thus evil is self-destructive.

Those who have known life and yet have exchanged The Truth for a lie have turned away from all that is GOD, all that is Good, and all that is Glory. Life has become lifeless, Light is exchanged for darkness, and Glory is exchanged for gloom. GOD has given these souls what they want, what they have desired, and what they have chosen.

To all who did it all, but thought to do it all without HIM, and never unto HIM, and never for HIM, who have no covenant with HIM, who have no intimacy with HIM, no union with HIM, or communion with HIM, they will never hear "enter The Joy of THE LORD". They only hear "depart, for you were never and did not ever choose to be a part of ME! You lived apart from ME, so depart from ME, for this is your will now being affirmed. You are choosing to continue to live apart from ME, in the lands of the shadows of death. Your will that you willed, is being done. This is your choice, these are your chains, this is your casket, and this is your living death from which you can never die. You have imprisoned yourself in hell by your own willful, stubborn, prideful, heart. You said "no" to GOD, you locked ME out, and thus yourself in. The door to your hell is locked on the inside, by you. Your LORD proclaims HIS Heart's greatest pain, when the day comes that your choice has brought this response, from HIM to you: "I never knew you. I have sought you, but you have hid. I have cried for you, but you have laughed at ME. I have died for you, but you have not died for ME. I have made covenant with you, but you have broken covenant with ME. I have sent you my angels, but you have chosen satan's.

I have sent you my prophets, but you have chosen false ones. I have sent you MY WORD, but you have chosen to live by your own words. I have sent you MY SON, MY ONLY ONE, but you rejected HIM, mocked HIM, ridiculed HIM, and murdered HIM. Yet I decided to make this, HIS death, your way back home. But you have chosen to make your own way to your own home. I am ever speaking throughout all Creation to you, calling you home, yet you choose to remain homeless. I have given you MY Heart, but you have rejected ME, and remain heartless. I have given you sight, but you choose to remain blind. I have made the ear, but you choose to remain deaf. I have given you everything, and yet you thank ME for nothing. I wait for you all the day, and yet you seek to be loved by another. I have given you all, but you have chosen to abuse all. There is no more to give, but to you, your own will. Depart from ME, for you are no part of ME."

This is The Heart of GOD. Little do people realize, less do most care, the pain GOD suffers when someone chooses to reject HIM. GOD suffers. GOD hurts. GOD knows it like no man can. Only GOD, being GOD, could handle the pain of the rejection by HIS Own. HE truly suffers the rejection of man. Being GOD, HE is capable of dealing with HIS Own Pain.

GOD is fair to all, giving to all essentially what they want. This is fair, even more than fair! This is freedom! Be careful how you use your freedom! Be careful what you choose, you may well get it.[20]

C: WHY DOES GOD CREATE JUNK, OR DOES HE?

Asking this question means that you think you're really bad, but you're not. GOD did not create you bad. GOD does not make junk! GOD loves you! HE has a Plan for your life, a good life, a productive life, a happy life! GOD Created you in HIS Image! You have so much going for you. See yourself through HIS Eyes. Trust in HIM. Give HIM your life! Let HIM take control. Give JESUS a chance. JESUS LOVES you!

[1]Matthew 7:13 [2]Romans 8:29 [3]Romans 8:30 [4]Ephesians 1:5 [5]Ephesians 1:11 [6]Romans 9:5 [7]Psalm 115:3 [8]Job 38:33 [9]Deuteronomy 10:17 [10]Jeremiah 29:11 [11]Deuteronomy 30:19,20 [12]Matthew 7:13,14 [13]John 3:36 [14]John 10:10 [15]Malachi 3:6a; James 1:17; Hebrews 13:8 [16]Micah 6:8; Ecclesiastes 12:13 [17]John 3:19,20

[18] 1 John 2:8 [19] *The Letters of John the Apostle* by Donald W. Burdick p144 [20] *Kings and Priests* Tape series—see **www.ForHISGlory.org/** catalog at **www.ForHISGlory.org** for details

GOD gives you what you want, since The Decision to choose has been given to you. HE has sovereignly given us sovereignty over our actions, choices, thoughts, and lives.

HE has told us what to do.[16] The decision is ours.
HE will *confirm* your decision, affirming your right to choose what you choose, but not choosing the choice for us. GOD gives you what you want.

[16]Micah 6:8; Ecclesiastes 12:13

9

DON'T ALL ROADS LEAD TO GOD?

A: Do you mean to tell me that people who have led good lives and served their fellow man well, but have denied JESUS as their LORD and SAVIOUR, are they going to hell?

In ultimate terms, you cannot be good when you deny GOD. GOD is the Source and the Author of all Goodness. To deny GOD is to deny Goodness its Source and its Expression as an essential attribute of GOD. Goodness without GOD is not Good, but merely a philosophical abstraction and an attempt at a "life principle" separated from its source, its power, and its strength. Like a limb severed from a tree, is goodness separated from GOD. One has the form of it in their very hand, but severed from the source of it. Therefore the life of the limb is no more what it once was meant to be in its essential nature, but has to be resuscitated with one's own thoughts and ideals, yet in an ever losing battle—as far from GOD as the Heavens are above the Earth.

Most importantly, is to see how JESUS views the matter: we look to[1] and we see a TORAH teacher asking JESUS: "What is the greatest commandment?"

JESUS answered and said: "Hear O Israel, THE LORD our GOD, THE LORD is ONE. And you shall love THE LORD your GOD with all your heart, with all your soul, and with all your strength. And you shall love your neighbor as yourself." JESUS said: "There is no other commandment greater than these"[2]

Note most importantly JESUS was asked what is the singular, most important commandment. Yet, strange as it might seem, the single most important commandment is, in effect, two. Well note, that one question was asked, but two answers were given. For both answers truly fulfill the most important commandment.

Further, THE LORD has said: "How can you say you love GOD WHOM you haven't seen, when you hate another whom you have seen? If a man says 'I love GOD' and hates his brother, he is a liar: for he that loves not his brother whom he has seen, how can he love GOD WHOM he has not seen?[3]

A very necessary and interesting revelation is a deeper meaning of the Hebrew word LOVE. It's grammatical root is ahav. When this root is well analyzed, it actually means THE FATHER revealed! Therefore, true love, in the Biblical, original and deeper sense of the word, means to reveal THE FATHER. The next question that follows is: "who can reveal THE FATHER?" Answer: "Only THE SON knows THE FATHER and everyone to whom THE SON chooses to reveal THE FATHER to."[4]

Therefore, the only way to know GOD THE FATHER is through GOD THE SON. Without THE SON of GOD, JESUS CHRIST, one does not have covenant. Without covenant, without JESUS, one cannot reveal THE FATHER. Therefore they cannot demonstrate love in the Biblical sense. Note well that JESUS says: "by this all men will know you are MY disciples, by how you love = reveal THE FATHER, one another."

B: DON'T ALL ROADS LEAD TO GOD?

Yes! All roads do lead to GOD. Every religion, every culture, every person, at every place in the world, in all times, throughout all of human history, will see GOD. Some consider Christianity to be an exclusivistic religion, in effect saying that they are the only way.

True Christianity says all roads lead to GOD, and so they do. One Road leads to GOD as both LORD and SAVIOUR, whereas all other roads lead to GOD as LORD and JUDGE. JESUS is at the head of both roads. Everyone will see JESUS whether they want to or not, whether they like it or not, and whether they believe it or not. Do you want to see JESUS as SAVIOUR, or do you want to see JESUS as JUDGE? The choice is yours. Remember, JESUS is LORD over all![5]

C: WHAT ABOUT THOSE WHO HAVE NEVER HEARD?

They have heard! Who told you they haven't heard?[6]

> For all who have sinned without THE TORAH will also perish without THE TORAH; and all who have sinned under THE TORAH will be judged by THE TORAH. For not the hearers of THE TORAH are just before GOD, but the doers of THE TORAH will be justified. For when gentiles (non-believers) who do not have THE TORAH do instinctively the things of THE TORAH, these not having THE TORAH are a TORAH unto themselves. In that they show the work of THE TORAH written in their hearts, their conscience bearing witness, and their thoughts alternately accusing or else defending them, on the day when, according to my GOSPEL, GOD will judge the secrets of men through JESUS CHRIST.
>
> — Romans 2:12-16

Stealing: where does the sense of wrong come about when someone steals from you? How do you know its wrong? Even a thief knows stealing is wrong.

Lying: you don't want to be lied to. Even when you lie, you know it's wrong.

Murder: how about murder? If someone murders someone you love, how do you know it's wrong? Where does this feeling come from? How do you know it's wrong?

GOD already wrote THE TRUTH on your heart and soul. That's how you know! JESUS HIMSELF said: "I came into the world that I might bear witness to THE TRUTH. Everyone who is of THE TRUTH hears my voice."[7]

[1]Mark 12:28-34 [2]Mark 12:31 [3]1 John 4:20 [4]Matthew 11:27 [5]Romans 9:5; Philippians 2:10; Isaiah 45:23; Revelation 1:7; Matthew 25:31-46 [6]Romans 2:12-16 [7]John 18:37b; cf: *NAMEs of GOD* Tape series on TRUTH (EMET).—see catalog at **www.ForHISGlory.org** for details

---

All roads lead to GOD.
One Road leads to GOD
as both LORD and *SAVIOUR,*
all other roads lead to GOD
as LORD and *JUDGE.*

10

I CAN'T UNDERSTAND HOW GOD COULD ALLOW MY LOVED ONE TO DIE.

A/B/C: I CAN'T UNDERSTAND HOW GOD COULD ALLOW MY FATHER (MOTHER, SON, DAUGHTER, ETC.) TO DIE. WHY?

GOD did not kill them, sin did... our sin![1] GOD has nothing to do with death. In fact, HE calls death (actually, THE death) the final enemy.[2] In point of fact, satan, the adversary, comes to steal, kill and destroy.[3] But JESUS came to give us life, and life more abundantly.

A common misconception, said in the anguish of the moment, is that "GOD took my child-loved one away because HE needs them in Heaven". Not only is this un-Biblical, it flies in the face of reason. For why would GOD send a soul into the world with a Divine Plan imprinted upon it: with hopes, dreams, aspirations, and the promise of long life to the Covenant-keeping one,[4] only to cut that life short, never fulfilling its purpose or its plan, merely to be brought back to Heaven, going back to where that soul was in the first place. There is no evidence of this Biblically, and it makes no sense reasonably.

Our consolation to those who so suffer is, The Truth: They are with GOD. They are in peace. They are home. And one day, by and by, we will be reunited with them again, forever, and never be separated, ever again. Thanks be to GOD!

[1]Romans 5:12; Romans 3:23; Romans 6:23
[2]1 Corinthians 15:26 [3]John 10:10 [4]Eph. 6:2,3

GOD did not kill them, sin did... our sin![1]
GOD has nothing to do with death. In fact, HE calls death (actually, <u>the</u> death) the final enemy.[2]

[1]Romans 5:12; Romans 3:23; Romans 6:23 [2]1 Cor. 15:26

11

WHY DOES THE BIBLE TELL ME TO BE JOYFUL WHEN BAD THINGS HAPPEN TO ME?

A/B: WHY DID GOD PUT ME IN THIS TRIAL? I DON'T LIKE IT! WHY DOES GOD TELL ME TO BE JOYFUL WHEN BAD THINGS HAPPEN TO ME? DOESN'T THE BIBLE SAY: "CONSIDER IT ALL JOY WHEN I FALL"?[1]

GOD didn't put you in this trial, period. First, please note carefully the initial tone of these verses[2]. We are told, "to consider it all joy…". It does not say "consider it all right or good." Did you get that? Please don't miss it; it is far too important, for its sets the tone for what is to follow. It tells us to adjust our attitude, not our theology. It tells us that our attitude should be one of joy, not that falling into trials is right at all.

Note the next few words[3] carefully: It says "to consider it all joy when <u>you</u> fall…". Did you note that? It says when <u>you</u> fall, it is <u>you</u> who caused the fall. For it is your action, your movement, your decision. It does not say GOD pushed you, GOD allowed you, GOD

49

wanted you to fall, etc. It merely says that you need an attitude adjustment when you make a mistake. Instead of walking with THE LORD, we walked away, we fell; the action is ours. Our initial response should be to be penitent to GOD for our fall, and to adjust our attitude through it, for GOD will work us through it until we're through with it, getting us back on our feet, standing strong, complete, lacking nothing.

Now, lets look at the word "trial", which in the Greek is the word *payrosmos*. This word, according to Nicoll[4] :

> "obviously means allurement to wrong doing and this would appear to be the most natural meaning here on account of the way in which temptation is analyzed, though the sense of external trials, in the shape of calamity, would of course not be excluded."

Continuing, "consider it all joy when you fall into various trials, knowing that <u>the approved part of your faith works endurance</u>" (this is the literal Greek translation). The word "approved"[5] *dokimion*:

> "according to instances of the use of the word *dokimion* given by Deissmann (Neue Bibelstudien, pp. 187ff.) it means "pure" or "genuine"; it is the neuter of the adjective used as a substantive, followed by a genitive; the phrase would thus mean: "That which is genuine in your faith worketh…"; This meaning of *dokimion* makes 1 Peter 1:7 clearer and more significant;".

Further, A.T. Robertson[6] says:

> "The proof (to *dokimion*). Now known (Deissmann, Bible Studies, pp. 259ff.) from the papyri examples of *dokimios* as an adjective in the same sense (good gold, standard gold) as *dokimos* proved or tested (James 1:12). The use of to *dokimion* (neuter article with neuter single adjective) here and in 1 Peter 1:7, clearly means "the genuine element in your faith," not "crucible" nor "proving." Your faith like gold stands the test of fire and is approved as standard.

James here, as in verse 6;2:1;5:15 regards faith (*pistis*) like Paul "as the very foundation of religion" (Mayor).

This supports what we said earlier.

There is a part of your faith, the approved/tried/tested part of your faith, that will help you endure. You are to know that your faith produces the endurance, and let that endurance have its perfect work, in order that you may be perfect, or mature, complete, in nothing lacking. That makes sense. When we fall into various trials, GOD tells us to consider it all joy, meaning, to keep your attitude right.

Don't sin twice; first by falling, second by having a fallen attitude with it. With the right attitude, your altitude will be higher. Then, that approved part of your faith will work endurance, bringing you as you work with it to a place of maturity and completeness in and with the issue at hand.

This is where we should have been before we fell. Nevertheless, GOD is always with you, and will never leave you or forsake you, because HE cannot deny HIMSELF.[7] An additional thought is to recognize the very next verse, which is just a continuation of the Letter, here, in context. It states "if any of you lacks/wants wisdom, let him ask from GOD, THE ONE giving to all men generously and without reproach, and it will be given to him."[8] Obviously, it would help the person who has fallen into various trials, to have the wisdom from GOD necessary so as not to fall.

Remember, in Hebrew, the concept of wisdom is not just information, but a practical skill that evidences wisdom in action in life.

A must connection is with 1 Peter 1:6,7. "In this you greatly rejoice, even though now for a little while, if necessary, you have been distressed by various trials, that the proof of your faith, being more precious than gold which is perishable, even though tested by fire, may be found to result in praise and glory and honor at the revelation of JESUS CHRIST:"

Now, isn't this sounding more like GOD? Most assuredly it does. For GOD is Good and HIS Loyal Love, HIS Lovingkindness endures forever.[9]

Let's look at the verse section: "In this you greatly rejoice, even though now, for a little while, if necessary, you have been distressed by various trials,..." Nicoll says[10]: "to take the 'necessity' as referring to their trials, (for not all the Saints are oppressed) limits the Greek term *lupathentes* = grieving to be external sense of vexation without reference to the feelings of the grieved corresponding to the feelings implied in *agalliasthe* = you exult = rejoice"

C: DOES GOD PUT ME THROUGH BAD THINGS IN ORDER TO MAKE ME A BETTER PERSON?

No! GOD does not put us through bad things in order to make us a better person. Remember you're speaking about GOD. Remember HIS Character! HE said that HE came to give us life and life more abundantly.[11] HE also said: "Beloved, I wish above all things that thou mayest prosper and be in health, even as thy soul prospers".[12] GOD has a plan to prosper us.[13] Remember HE is a Good GOD! Bad things do happen to good people, but that is not HIS Will or Desire. HE has given us Sovereignty and HE has given us everything we need to learn without having to suffer first in order to learn it.[14]

There is a devil lurking around trying to tempt us. However, we ourselves make bad choices when we ignore GOD's Plan for us. We usually blame GOD when bad things happen and ignore our own responsibility. Our responsibility is our response to HIS Ability.

[1]James 1:2-4 [2]James 1:2 [3] cf. James 1:2 [4]*Expositors of the Greek New Testament,* Vol 4 ed. Robertson Nicoll, p421 [5]*Expositor's Greek Testament* Vol 4 ed. Robertson Nicoll p421 [6]A.T. Robertson's *Word Pictures in the New Testament* Vol 6, p12 [7]2 Timothy 2:13 [8]James 1:5 [9] Psalm 136:1 [10]*Expositor's Greek Testament* Vol 5 ed. Robertson Nicoll p43 [11]John 10:10 [12]1 John 3:2 [13]Jeremiah 29:11 [14]Romans 8:32 [15]from a sermon by Pastor Adrian Rogers

---

GOD is always with you, and will never leave you or forsake you; HE ever remains Faithful even when we are faithless, because HE cannot deny HIMSELF.[7]

[7]2 Timothy 2:13

12

WHAT ABOUT DEATH?

A: DEATH; THE WORTHLESS EXPERIENCE.

Death, the universal experience, the consummate thief. Experienced by all, and hated by most. It is ever common, but never correct. It continues to be a horrid reminder of the Great Fall of mankind. For death is the proof-text experience of the Biblical view that sin entered into the world through one man, and thus death through sin, thus death has spread to all men, because all have sinned.[1]

Death's children have names: disease, sickness, illness, pain, problems, emotional upheavals, mental aberrations, heaviness of soul, fear, and guilt, to name a few. These likewise steal, kill, and destroy lives in a wide variety of ways. You can read pain and suffering on someone's face and soul like a map on a page. It all goes in the wrong direction, it all comes from a wrong place.

Death destroys, death demolishes, and death murders the life that could have been, should have been, ought to have been, but never was, when death knocked on its door with an iron grip separating us from the source of life itself.

Sin, the father of death, entered sinless humanity through Adam and has cloaked us in an entropic spin ever away from life, headed straight towards a GODless, lifeless eternity in hell. Each spirit is repelled at the concept of sin and its son, death. satan, the father of lies, attempts to lure us into sin by craft and temptation. The unaware soul, the unregenerate spirit, can and has all too often fallen prey to satan's lies, thus becoming bound to the domain of darkness, in which sin and sickness and death reign.

For this purpose, the SON OF GOD was manifested, that HE might destroy the works of satan.[2] GOD would then transfer us from the domain of darkness into the Kingdom of THE SON of HIS LOVE.[3]

Through HIM WHO tasted death for everyone,[4] we have been given access once again to GOD THE FATHER, through HE HIM- SELF WHO IS THE WAY, THE TRUTH and THE LIFE, no one coming to THE FATHER except HIS WAY.[5]

Surely HE has borne all our sicknesses and sorrows, and carried all our pain.[6] HE was pierced through for our transgressions, HE was crushed for our iniquities, the chastening for our peace was upon HIM, and by HIS Wound, HE was healed for us. (literal translation of Isaiah 53:5)

Thus, HE has borne all our sicknesses; therefore you need not, nor should not. HE has borne all our pain; you need not, nor should not.

HE has carried away all our pain; you need not, nor should not. Since HE was pierced through for our transgressions, your debt has been paid in full. HE was crushed for our iniquities, thus removing from us the bent toward evil due to The Fall.

The price for our peace was paid by HIM, piece by piece. You need not be in lack when HE is your missing Piece-Peace. HIS Wound, that expressed HIS Life Blood, the very Blood of Life, paid the price in full for your life, for your blood.

HE took all our sin, sickness, disease, and death upon HIMSELF, simultaneously off us and our accounts.[7] Then, HE Healed HIMSELF and gave us a Healed, Whole, Holy Life in HIMSELF, the LAST ADAM, even greater than that which was lost in the First ADAM. GLORY to HIS NAME! There is no concord between THE SON OF GOD and satan, between Good and evil, between Right and wrong, or between Life and death.[8]

The saint of GOD should be sinless, sickless, and deathless. Sin should have no part or place in the believer. Sickness should have no place in the life of a believer. Death has no place in life, thus death has no place in the life of a believer. Death is an enemy,[9] the last great enemy, and all its children, all of which were abolished at the cross, their sentence pronounced: "IT IS FINISHED"![10]

We are to live in the realm of Truth, walking in THE SPIRIT, obeying The Law of The Spirit of Life in CHRIST JESUS, which has set us free from the law of sin and death.[11]

[1]Romans 5:12 [2]1 John 3:8b [3]Colossians 1:13 [4]Hebrews 2:9 [5]John 14:6 [6]Isaiah 53:4 [7]Romans 4:25 [8]2 Corinthians 6:15 [9]1 Corinthians 15:26 [10]John 19:30 [11]Romans 8:2

For this purpose,
THE SON OF GOD
was manifested,
that HE might destroy
the works of satan.[2]
GOD would then transfer
us from the domain of
darkness into the
Kingdom of
THE SON
of HIS LOVE.[3]

[2] 1 John 3:8b
[3] Colossians 1:13

13

WHAT ABOUT THE REALLY BAD GUYS?

A: WHAT ABOUT THE REALLY BAD GUYS? DOESN'T GOD LOVE THEM TOO?

Yes. GOD Loves them. GOD Loves us all. In GOD's Eyes, all have sinned, and all need a SAVIOUR.[1] For all have sinned and come short of the Glory of GOD. [2] The wages of sin is death, but the gift of GOD is eternal life in JESUS CHRIST our LORD.[3] Thus all are under the sentence of death in Adam, for it is destined for man to die once,[4] and all have, in the first Adam. Thus, all are headed toward a Final Judgment, a second death.[5] However, those who believe in JESUS CHRIST as LORD <u>and</u> SAVIOUR shall not come into Judgment but have passed from death to life.[6]

This choice, to believe, or not to believe, is a sovereign right given to mankind by ALMIGHTY GOD. GOD, in HIS Great Love, desires people to love HIM, not by force, nor by compulsion, but by choice. We too, in our human relationships, know that a love freely given is a true love indeed. A love that is forced, demanded, or mandated, is not a love, but an obligation, a duty, a coercion. This kind of love is a lie.

And that's the Truth! GOD demonstrated HIS Love to us, in that while we were yet sinners, CHRIST died for us.[7] So now let us come to HIM, and choose freely to love HIM.[8]

[1]Luke 13:1-5 [2]Romans 3:23 [3]Romans 6:23 [4]Hebrews 9:27
[5]Revelation 20:11-15; Revelation 2:11 [6]John 5:24 [7]Romans 5:8
[8]Matthew 10:39; Matthew 16:24-26

> # Yes. GOD Loves them.
> ## GOD Loves us all. But, in GOD's Eyes, all have sinned, and all need a SAVIOUR.[1]
> ## For all have sinned and come short of the Glory of GOD.[2]
>
> [1]Luke 13:1-5 [2]Romans 3:23

14

WHO's IN CHARGE?

A: WHO's IN CHARGE?

GOD is! GOD is LORD! THE LORD is in The Heavens; HE does whatever HE pleases.[1] THE LORD is KING of KINGs and LORD of LORDs. HE is The Great and The Mighty and The Awesome GOD[2] THE LORD sits enthroned as KING Forever.[3] The Heavens, and the Heaven of Heavens cannot contain GOD.[4] THE LORD Reigns![5]

Recognize that GOD, WHO IS SOVEREIGN, has sovereignly given us sovereignty over our wills, choices, and lives.

HE is still Sovereign, but now we have a derived sovereignty that gives us rights and abilities. Thus <u>we are responsible</u> for what we are able to do, whether we do it or not.[6] It is our choice!

[1]Psalm 115:3 [2]Deuteronomy 10:17
[3]Psalm 29:10 [4]I Kings 8:27 [5]Psalm 97:1
[6]Psalm 115:16; Matthew 25:14-30

WHO's in Charge?
GOD is! GOD is LORD!
THE LORD is in
The Heavens;
HE does
whatever HE pleases.[1]

[1]Psalm 115:3

15

CAN I UNDERSTAND GOD AT ALL?

A: DOESN'T SCRIPTURE CLEARLY TEACH US THAT "AS HIGH AS THE HEAVENS ARE ABOVE THE EARTH", SO "HIS WAYS ARE HIGHER THAN OUR WAYS AND HIS THOUGHTS ARE HIGHER THAN OUR THOUGHTS"?

Yes, but much more. A careful reading of the Chapter will make it patently clear that this verse could in no wise apply to a believer in THE LORD JESUS CHRIST. Further, the Text elucidates for us who the subject is relative to the verse in question.

The answer is in verse 7 (of Isaiah 55) "the wicked, unrighteous man". With respect to the wicked, unrighteous man, his thoughts truly are not GOD's Thoughts and his ways are obviously not GOD's Ways. For they are of the flesh and the Fall, and not of THE SPIRIT. They are of the Earth, not of the Heavens.

B: I know that GOD works in mysterious ways because GOD's Ways are not man's ways and GOD's Thoughts are not man's thoughts. Isn't that right?

No! That's a common misconception, not Biblical thought. Often you will hear an out-of-context quote along these lines: The BIBLE says: "For MY Thoughts are not your thoughts, nor MY Ways your ways", says THE LORD.[2] This statement is TRUTH, yet it is True for some, and not True for others. This is the key point, context. Often missed in the course of one's studies, people violate the common rule of grammar of taking a text out of context and making a pretext out of it, thus developing a thought foreign to its original, true meaning. We have only to go back one verse[3] and see whom GOD is really speaking to.

This happens to work here just as easily in a good English translation as in the original Hebrew Text. Starting back just one verse, we immediately see the subject being the wicked, unrighteous man, not the good and righteous man. GOD says "Let the wicked forsake his way and the unrighteous man his thoughts…" Read this very carefully. You will see the parallel concepts of way and thoughts of the wicked being strongly contrasted with the Ways and Thoughts of GOD.

Read slowly. The context clearly defines the subjects involved. Nowhere in these verses do you see the righteous man, the believer, a saint of GOD mentioned at all. So why do you apply them to yourself when it doesn't apply to you? If you are a righteous person, having the righteousness of CHRIST[4], then this Text[5] does not apply to you.

If you are a good person, and a Godly person, then this Text does not apply to you. If you are a wicked person, this Text applies to you. If you are an unrighteous person, this Text applies to you. However, hold on, there is hope for you. Just keep reading. "And let him return to THE LORD, and HE will have mercy upon him, and to our GOD, for HE will abundantly pardon."[6] There is Hope for you in THE LORD; there is Mercy for you in THE LORD, as long as you return to THE LORD. You must do this as honestly, and faithfully as you can. HE knows your heart. Remember what THE LORD said just one verse earlier: "Seek THE LORD while HE may be found, call upon HIM while HE is near."[7]

Now for the rest of you, who do know GOD, know GOD better. This Text has nothing to do with you. You have the "mind of Christ."[8] JESUS also told Thomas "you know the way where I am going"[9] Paul also records "As you have received CHRIST JESUS THE LORD, walk in HIM"[10] An interesting perspective is in[11] Deuteronomy 11:28 where GOD tells us that we "will bring a curse" on our own head "if we don't obey The Commandments of THE LORD our GOD but turn aside from the Way which GOD commanded us this day, going after other gods which we have not known."

Study this carefully, that to turn aside from The Way means that we knew The Way from which we were warned not to turn away from, and going after other gods, which we have not known. This is a turning away from THE GOD WHOM we have known.

The sum of the matter is this: you know GOD, you know HIS Ways, and you know HIS Thoughts. You are HIS Body, you are HIS Bride if you are a Christian, and you are the family of GOD. To know GOD's Ways and Thoughts does not mean that you know all there is to know about GOD, or ever will. But THE GOD you do know, is consistent with those things of GOD we don't yet or ever will know, because you have come to know the Character of GOD which does not change.[12]

C: HOW CAN I MAKE SENSE OF ANY OF THIS AT ALL?

GOD is Good. HE is telling you what to do. Look for HIM and do it now. GOD is not talking about the righteous man, the Christian. HE is talking about bad people—their ways are not GOD's Ways and their thoughts are not GOD's Thoughts. So this does not apply to the righteous man.

There is an answer for the bad people, no matter how bad they are.—JESUS is THE ANSWER! Look to HIM, be straight with HIM, and to-the-bone honest. Come as you are. Ask HIM to change you, to fix you, to give you a new start. And HE will! HE promises to give you a new start, another chance, a renewed purpose in life. HE will make sense of it all for you.

[1]Isaiah 55:9 [2]Isaiah 55:8 [3]Isaiah 55:7 [4]2 Corinthians 5:21 [5]Isaiah 55:9 [6]Isaiah 55:7 [7]Isaiah 55:6 [8]1 Corinthians 2:16 [9]John 14:4 [10]Colossians 2:6 [11]Deuteronomy 11:28 [12]Malachi 3:6a; Hebrews 13:8; James 1:17

To know GOD's Ways and Thoughts does not mean that you know all there is to know about GOD, or ever will. But THE GOD you do know, is consistent with those things of GOD we don't yet or ever will know, because you have come to know the Character of GOD which does not change.[12]

[12]Malachi 3:6a; Hebrews 13:8; James 1:17

16

HOW DO I PRAY?

Remember, from Chapter 5B: *Why Don't My Prayers Work?*, that Prayer changes you, not GOD. GOD does not change.[1] Also recall that the Hebrew verb for "to pray" in primarily reflexive, meaning that the subject *acts upon itself*. Thus prayer changes you. How much does GOD want you to pray? HE wants you to pray all the time; without ceasing.[2]

Question: Why? Answer: because we need to change, and change constantly, growing to the measure of the stature that belongs to the fullness of CHRIST.[3] Prayer enables us to change continually and continuously, becoming more and more like JESUS when HE was on Earth. HE is our Elder Brother, Bone of our bone and Flesh of our flesh. Prayers work to the degree you pray. To the degree you work prayer, prayer will work you. You can well become the answer of your own prayer.

Study prayer deeply. It is a science whose depth has no parallel in the natural sciences. It is a science of GOD that needs to be approached with the greatest severity, the greatest diligence, and the greatest sincerity. Do not pray for an answer, pray believing that you have received it already and it will be given you.[5] We think so often in linear time, not unlike the rest of the world. We live today, we remember yesterday, and we hope and plan for tomorrow. Likewise, we pray wrongly. We let our past color our thoughts and thus narrow our prayers. We let present circumstances create a sense of lack in our lives from which we then pray for the lack to be met and our needs to be satisfied. Why then, does David say, "THE LORD is my Shepherd, I shall not lack"? [6] Why then, does the psalmist say, "I was young, and now I am old, yet I have not seen the righteous forsaken, nor his descendants begging bread?"[7] Why then, does the psalmist say, "THE LORD GOD is a Sun and Shield, THE LORD will give you Grace and Glory—no good thing does HE withhold from those who walk uprightly?"[8] Why then, does Isaiah say, "The path of the righteous is uprightness, O Upright ONE, YOU make the path of the righteous smooth?"[9]

Thus the path of the just (those right with GOD) is a level way. That is, GOD makes it orderly, upright, and straight toward its goal. We need some direction then, don't we? Yes, we do. Question: What direction should we take? Answer: look where GOD looks. Seek where GOD seeks. And, that is in the past. Note carefully,[10] "That which is has been already. And that which will be, has already been, for GOD seeks what has passed by." Notice carefully, *that* which is, *that* being the present, is Biblically, technically, in the past. Further, *that* which will be, that being the future, is also Biblically, technically, in the past.

Note carefully, the present and the future are not only rooted in the past, they *coexist* in the past. Therefore, since GOD HIMSELF seeks what is passed by, does it not behoove us likewise to look where HE looks, and seek what HE seeks? Else, it seems to me that we often pass GOD like two ships in the night, going in the opposite direction from HIM, trying ever harder, yet going ever farther from HIM. No wonder so many have cried out to GOD for answers, yet, they are asking the wrong questions. Better to first ask like the psalmist: "LORD, teach me YOUR Ways, make me know YOUR Paths". [11] Further, look to walk like a Moses did, who knew HIS Ways whereas the children of Israel just saw HIS Acts.[12]

You are a citizen of Heaven.[13] In Heaven there is no lack. You are heirs of GOD and joint heirs with CHRIST.[14] You have access to all that belongs to an heir and joint- heir, according to the Plan of GOD, to establish the Kingdom of GOD and bring Heaven to Earth. Walk, live, and be like a child of the KING. Pray as a citizen of Heaven, who already has all the rights and privileges and blessings of Heavenly citizenship. Don't ask for what you already have as a joint heir unless you ask believing that you already have it! [15] Walk out your life that GOD has already worked out.[16]

Too many look for the path and not the Light. Too many look to find themselves instead of lose themselves for HIS sake. The life we find without HIM will destroy us. The life we give to HIM for HIS sake will cause us to find True Life, True Meaning, and Truth. Speak like GOD's own. Walk, clothed in CHRIST. Be complete in HIM. Your prayers should speak truth, life, completion, and Heaven into manifestation. Revelation brings illumination that by application you can bring into manifestation for HIS Glorification! Keep praying right. Your life will change into HIS.

[1]Malachi 3:6a, James 1:17, Hebrews 13:8

[2]1 Thessalonians 5:17 [3]Ephesians 4:13

[5]Mark 11:24 [6]Psalm 23:1 [7]Psalm 37:25

[8]Psalm 84:11 [9]Isaiah 26:7 [10]Ecclesiastes 3:15

[11]Psalm 25:4 [12] Psalm 103:7 [13]Philippians 3:20

[14]Romans 8:17 [15]Mark 11:24; Matthew 7:7,8

[16]Ephesians 2:10; Psalm 119:105

Pray as a citizen of Heaven,
who already has all the rights
and privileges and blessings
of Heavenly citizenship.
Don't ask for what you already
have as a joint-heir unless you
ask believing that you
already have it![15]

[15]Mark 11:24; Matthew 7:7,8

17

SINCE WE ARE FALLEN, DON'T WE ALWAYS SIN? IS A CHRISTIAN A SINNER OR A SAINT? CAN A CHRISTIAN BE SINLESS?

Yes! JESUS was. JESUS was the first Christian. HE was sinless in all HIS Ways, every day and every night. Thus, as a Sinless Sacrifice, HE was able to take all our sin and punishment due, and atone for it through HIS Flesh and Blood Sacrifice. We are saved from sin, and the *proclivity* (a bend/tendency) to sin. HE has delivered us not only from sin, but also from the *power* of sin. Thus the Christian has been enabled to walk as JESUS walked, because of JESUS. Now we can walk out sinlessly what HE has worked out selflessly. John records that he has written to us what THE MASTER has commanded, in order that we do not sin.[1]

In John 8, JESUS tells the woman caught in adultery, "Neither do I condemn you; go your way. From now on sin no more."[2] And THE LORD GOD ALMIGHTY told Abraham "walk before ME and be blameless."[3]

JESUS has saved us from sin, not to sin. Further, the Power of GOD fully enables the believer to walk free from sin, sickness, and satan in all it's varied forms and at all times. The Gospel, to quote John G. Lake, is "a strong man's Gospel." It brings Good News to the afflicted, it has power to bind the brokenhearted, through it we proclaim liberty to the captives and freedom to the prisoners."[4]

An important distinction to make here is that, if we're honest, too often *we do not believe what we just prayed.* Our prayers are more wishful and hopeful, than believable. This will not do. We are told to pray believing.[5] The success of your prayer life would markedly increase if you spent the necessary time during and after each and every prayer, totally believing what you just said.

Remember Abraham, who, having received the Promise of GOD of a future heir, a son, though the physical evidence of his and his wife's body gave no evidence to this being possible. But he believed.[6] He did not waver in unbelief. This is what we would call doubt. Doubt must be destroyed in your mind, and in your prayers. Doubt creates a wavering of faith, a weakening of faith, and a breaking of the bridge that your prayer was forming from your heart to HIS.

GOD has already established a perfect connection from HIM to us through JESUS CHRIST. JESUS CHRIST is THE HIGH PRIEST of our confession [7]. What is confession? Basically the word confession is formed from two Greek words: *homo* and *legei* = same word. Thus confession would be to say the same thing/word. JESUS CHRIST is THE HIGH PRIEST of our confession, bringing the words that we speak on Earth to THE FATHER as our HIGH PRIEST when those words are an acceptable sacrifice by a priest or priestess (you). Those words must be acceptable before the Throne of Heaven to be brought to Heaven by our HIGH PRIEST. We must speak the same words as GOD over any situation for those words to be empowered by GOD, which they will be when they are HIS Words that HE has Spoken and is Watching over to Perform.[8] Thus once you have prayed the prayer of faith[9] over the problem, having spoken to GOD about the problem, you are now in agreement with HIM as to the solution for the problem. Now, continue to thank GOD for the solution to the problem, continuing to speak to the problem what GOD has said and already done. This was brought home to me by James Roberson in his book *The Walk of the Spirit The Walk of Power.*

[1]1John 2:1 [2]John 8:11 [3]Genesis 17:1
[4]Isaiah 61:1 [5]Mark 11:24 [6]Romans 4:19
[7]Hebrews 3:1 [8]Jeremiah 1:12; Isaiah 55:11
[9]James 5:15 (verses 13,14 for context)

In **John 8**, JESUS tells the woman caught in adultery, "Neither do I condemn you; go your way. From now on sin no more."[2]

[2]John 8:11

18

WHY BOTHER? ISN'T GOD ON HIS THRONE?

The force of this question leads one to believe that because GOD is on HIS Throne, everything is all right. This needs more careful thought. To say: "GOD is on HIS Throne" as a response to some difficult or even horrible situation leads one quickly to a wrong conclusion. This being that because "GOD is on HIS Throne," the situation is either all right or will be all right.

Many situations are not all right, and have never turned out all right, period. For every drunk driver that has turned their life around and done good, there are hundreds that have gone from bad to worse, wreaking untold havoc to themselves and an ever increasing number of others.

In some families, the husband is never coming home. In other families, the children's room is perpetually empty. They are dead, not returning to the land of the living. For every child that has left home, and returned like a prodigal, at times the better, there are an untold number who never return home. They walk the streets, live in the rat-infested sewers, or live the hell of forced prostitution and slavery by the millions around the world.

For every lost soul that comes to the Knowledge of the Glory of GOD in the Face of the MESSIAH JESUS, there are others who have turned from light to dark, from Heaven to hell, from life to death, to live dead forever in the land of perpetual darkness. This is never good.

However, evil has been comprehended and apprehended in the overarching Plan of GOD. HE has set limits to evil. It is self-defeating and self-destroying (see Chapter 8B) It will ultimately be judged and done away with.[1] Good will triumph. Good people will finish first. Right makes might. GOD *is* on HIS Throne. The question is not "Is GOD on HIS Throne?", but *"are we on ours?"*[2]

[1]Revelation 20:11-15
[2]Daniel 7:9; Revelation 4:4; Psalm 122:5

The question is *not* "Is GOD on HIS Throne?", but "are we on ours?"[2]

[2]Daniel 7:9; Revelation 4:4; Psalm 122:5

19

WHAT ABOUT THE REALLY GOOD PEOPLE? WHAT HAPPENS TO THEM? DO THEY GO TO HEAVEN?

An interesting question. Let's examine it carefully. I would like you to imagine that you are the owner of a large estate, with property, possessions, and nearly limitless resources. You have a child, whom you loved from the first, even before they were born. They grew up in your house with everything available to them, with an ever-caring father who has supplied every need and made provision for every eventuality in that child's life.

The child grows. For reasons only known to the child, he turns his back on his father. Spurning his love, he ignores his dad. When they talk, the child is rude and abrasive, developing stubbornness to the core. The child refuses to have a relationship with his father, living his own life, doing his own thing. The rejection experienced by the father, the pain of separation felt by the father, the dreams that could have and should have been of a life together, father and son, parent and child, have been ripped asunder, torn in two, by the child's own hands and actions. Yet that person's very life was torn apart from GOD by his own hands. He separated himself from GOD, thus turning his back on GOD, Heaven, and Good.

Is this a good child? Is this a good man? Though the world would look at him and see a great giver, he gave away what didn't belong to him. The world looked at him as a great leader, but he never led them to GOD. The world looked at him as extremely talented, but he did not acknowledge the talent as from GOD. The world sees a good man, but GOD sees no one. How can this man be any good? He stole from his father; he used his father's things without asking. He could care less about how his dad felt about anything or even what he said. He ignores his dad, but acts like the owner of the house. He drives his dad's car, uses his dad's money, and uses his dad's abilities, all for himself, only for himself. That's selfish. That's prideful. That's spiteful. That's wrong. Would you call this man good? GOD doesn't. GOD says: "I never knew you, because you left ME forever. Depart from ME, for you never were a part of ME. Continue in the direction of your own choosing; alone, without ME."

This child left but didn't leave. He hasn't gone, but he's gone.

> The world looks to some as great leaders, but they do not lead people to GOD. The world looks at some as extremely talented, but they do not acknowledge their talent as from GOD. The world sees a good man, but GOD sees no one.

20

DO PEOPLE SUFFER?

Yes they do! In 1 Peter 4:12 and the following verses[1],…these "fiery ordeals" come upon you for trial (an allurement to evil, even the external event of calamity)…"as though some strange thing were happening to you" = common occurrence…that to the degree you rejoice just as you share the sufferings of CHRIST in order that also at the revelation of HIS Glory, you may rejoice exulting…It can't be sin or anything related to sin, or as a result of sin, for all sin has been dealt with at the Cross of CHRIST, in HIS Body, and HIS Blood.

Therefore: sin, sickness, disease, transgressions, inequities, and all that is in opposition to GOD, and opposing HIS Will, is sin, for which the penalty has been fully paid through the Blood and Body of THE LORD JESUS CHRIST at the Cross of Calvary.

Therefore we rejoice in the sufferings of CHRIST (v 15), not in the sin of man. We are not to rejoice when we suffer the consequences for our own sin, for GOD is grieved and so should we be. There is provision for release from our sin due to the atonement of CHRIST and HIS *full payment* at the Cross in HIS Body and Blood. CHRIST was persecuted not by sin, but by sinners. CHRIST did no evil, but evil was done to HIM. CHRIST became sin for us, that we might become the righteousness of GOD in HIM[2].

Therefore there is no good in a righteous person sinning, and suffering the effects of sin. This is then *not* what the Text is addressing. It talks about the unfortunate commonality of the fierce-fiery ordeal, among you, which is the all-too-frequent experience for the Christian. This word for trial in the Greek is: *payrasmon* according to Nicoll[3]:

> "obviously means allurement to wrong doing and this would appear to be the most natural meaning here (James 1:2) on account of the way in which temptation is analyzed, though the sense of external trials, in the shape of calamity, would of course not be excluded."

This could *not* be sin, sickness, wrong-doing, iniquity, etc. because CHRIST, being our sin-bearer, and taking the iniquity of all, has paid the price for us all.[4] We are told to "rejoice in the sufferings of CHRIST" so that we may rejoice exultingly at HIS Revelation. Therefore there must be something very positive about the "sufferings of CHRIST" which will result in exuberant rejoicing when HE returns. What could that be?

Continuing, in verses 14-16, if you are reproached in the NAME of CHRIST, you are blessed because the SPIRIT of Glory and of GOD rests upon you. But by no means, let not any of you suffer as a murderer, or a thief, or evil-doer, or a troublesome-meddler, or as a pryer into other men's affairs; but if as a Christian, let him not be shamed, for let him glorify GOD by this NAME.

What does "in the NAME of CHRIST" mean? "In the NAME of CHRIST" means "in the essence of", "within the nature of". Therefore, if you are reproached in the NAME of CHRIST, you're being reproached because you are operating in the nature of CHRIST as one of HIS very own. Therefore you share the sufferings of CHRIST. Just as HE was reproached for WHO HE was, and you being HIS Body, and HIS Bride, are one with HIM and in HIM, therefore we also share the same persecutions and reviling. Evil still does evil, hate still hates, many are still at war with GOD, and in total rebellion, even though peace has been declared by GOD. Reconciliation has been made by

GOD through CHRIST.[5] You can come home now, and be at home and at peace with GOD, and in yourself.[6]

The common mistake is to construe the "trials" as tests from GOD as opposed to allurements to evil and calamities from satan himself. If we are enticed by our own lusts to sin, then that sin will eventually lead to death: ours! [7] Therefore the suffering that is undergone by the Christian in 1 Peter 5:8,9 is somehow intrinsically related contextually to the attack of satan. We are told to stand firm in The Faith.[8] We are told that CHRIST always leads us to triumph[9] (but we must follow HIS leading to walk in the triumph of CHRIST.) Note carefully, that the same Greek term for sufferings[10] *pathaamaton* is used in the same Epistle of Peter for the sufferings of CHRIST *pathaamasin*. The conclusion is linear and complete. The sufferings of the brethren throughout the whole world are due to satanic attacks, which are of the same quality as the sufferings of CHRIST. This is very important to note. We do rejoice in the fact that you are a Christian, operating in the essence of CHRIST. Therefore, this suffering is happening *because*, satan is not happy with you and therefore attacks you in the same way he attacked CHRIST, though there was no sin in HIM. So when satan attacks you and you are reviled and reproached and suffer as a Christian, in THE NAME of CHRIST, in the Essence of CHRIST, rejoice because, here, sin has no hold on you, sickness has no place in you, iniquity has no home in you, even transgression does not walk with you. You will therefore emerge victorious, an over-comer through Faith in THE SON of GOD, and you will be rewarded for having kept The Faith, standing firm in The Faith, holding up the shield of Faith, and extinguishing all the flaming arrows of the evil one. You stand in CHRIST's Victory as more than a conqueror. In this you re-present (represent) HIM well.[9]

[1] 1 Peter 4:12 "Beloved, do not think it strange concerning the fiery trial..." [2] 2 Corinthians 5:21

[3] *Expositors of the Greek New Testament*, Vol 4 ed. Robertson Nicoll, p421 [4] Isaiah 53:4,5,12

[5] 2 Corinthians 5:18 [6] 1 Peter 5:8,9

[7] James 1:13-16 [8] 1 Peter 5:9

[9] 2 Corinthians 2:14; 2 Corinthians 5:20

> # The common mistake is to construe the "trials" as tests from GOD, as opposed to allurements to evil and calamities from satan himself. If we are enticed by our own lusts to sin, then that sin will eventually lead to death: ours![7]
>
> **[7]James 1:13-16**

Thank you for joining us on the road to TRUTH! We pray this book has been a Blessing to you as much as it has been for us.

The For HIS Glory Ministry is a non-profit organization, without denominational affiliation. It's mission statement is drawn from The Biblical Text in John 12:21, which states:

"We wish to see JESUS."

The ministry website is
<u>www.ForHISGlory.org</u>

and contains information on dozens of tape series and radio shows covering a wide range of various Biblical topics. The teachings are deep in scope, Hebraic and revelatory. They will challenge you, and equip you ever better to do the work of GOD.

The Ministry mailing address is:

For HIS Glory
2183 Buckingham Road, Suite 145
Richardson, Texas 75081

This book and all our materials can be ordered directly from our fulfillment center:

The Connextion
1-866-42ORDER (426-7337)

It is our sincere desire that either through this book and/or through our other teachings, you will be able to see GOD more clearly, love HIM more dearly, and worship HIM more sincerely, in SPIRIT and in TRUTH; for such true worshipers THE FATHER seeks.

WHY, GOD?

WHAT IS THE MEANING OF LIFE?
WHERE ARE YOU GOD?
THE SOVEREIGNTY OF GOD,
THE SOVEREIGNTY OF MAN;
ARE BOTH TRUE?
DO I NEED TO BE SICK, SAD,
OR SUFFER, TO BE A SAINT?
DOES GOD "ALLOW" BAD THINGS TO HAPPEN?
DOES A SOVEREIGN GOD PERMIT
BAD THINGS TO HAPPEN, OR DO WE?
HOW COULD A GOOD GOD CREATE PEOPLE
KNOWING
THAT MANY WOULD BE LOST IN HELL
FOREVER?
DON'T ALL ROADS LEAD TO GOD?
I CAN'T UNDERSTAND HOW GOD COULD
ALLOW MY LOVED ONE TO DIE.
WHY DOES THE BIBLE TELL ME TO BE JOYFUL
WHEN BAD THINGS HAPPEN TO ME?
WHAT ABOUT DEATH?
WHAT ABOUT THE REALLY BAD GUYS?
CAN I UNDERSTAND GOD AT ALL?
HOW DO I PRAY?
CAN A CHRISTIAN BE SINLESS?
WHY BOTHER? ISN'T GOD ON HIS THRONE?
WHAT ABOUT THE REALLY GOOD PEOPLE?
DO PEOPLE SUFFER?

0-595-23669-3